GW01017950

HEALTH FOR LIFE

low-fat
for kids

JODY VASSALLO

FORTIORI

LOW-FAT EATING FOR CHILDREN AND TEENAGERS

A healthy diet and regular physical activity are essential for children to reach their full physical and mental potential. Poor dietary habits and insufficient physical activity can adversely affect a child's ability to keep up with his or her peers both in and out of the classroom. Children learn by example. So if you teach your children the pleasures of eating well and exercising regularly fairly early in life by following these habits yourself, your children will find it easier to maintain a healthy lifestyle as they get older. Healthy lifestyle habits can also help protect your children against common nutrition-related diseases, such as obesity, heart disease and type-2 diabetes, that can start developing in childhood.

The information in this book is intended for parents of healthy children aged 7 years and older. It contains general advice about healthy eating and weight control, as well as a range of delicious recipes that are consistent with this advice. The recipes are easy to follow so that parents and children can enjoy preparing them together.

The information in this book should not replace any advice given to you by a doctor or dietitian. If your child has a specific health problem or appears to be overweight or underweight, consult a doctor and a dietitian before making any changes to his or her diet.

**Dr Susanna Holt
(PhD, dietitian)**

DIETARY RECOMMENDATIONS

1 | Children need healthy food and regular physical activity to grow and develop properly. Growth should be checked regularly and a healthy weight should be maintained.
2 | Their diet should contain a wide variety of nutritious foods.
3 | Meals and snacks should be based on grain products, vegetables and fruit.
4 | Low-fat diets are not suitable for children under 5 years; for older children a diet low in fat, particularly saturated fat, is appropriate.
5 | Children should be encouraged to drink plenty of water.
6 | Only moderate amounts of sugar and foods and drinks with added sugar should be eaten.
7 | Foods containing calcium and iron should be eaten regularly.
8 | Choose low-salt foods and don't add table salt to meals.
(Adapted from: Dietary guidelines for children and adolescents. National Health and Medical Research Council, Canberra, 1994.)

DIETARY PROBLEMS

Some common dietary problems that affect children and teenagers include:
| skipping main meals
| eating too many fast foods and snacks and not enough fruit and vegetables
| eating too many processed foods
| drinking calories rather than eating them (soft drinks, shakes, cordial, juice)
| not eating enough foods rich in iron, zinc and calcium
| eating too many calories and not being active enough.

HOW MUCH FOOD?

The appetite of a healthy, normal-weight child is usually the best gauge of how much they need to eat. In general, children and teenagers are hungrier during growth spurts when their body needs more energy. Children are growing and developing from birth until the end of puberty. Growth rates vary with age, and tend to occur in spurts. After the age of two, a child's rate of growth slows down until they reach puberty, when height and appetite both increase considerably.

Children generally need 3 meals and 2 to 3 snacks throughout the day. If your child is healthy and growing normally, you can leave it up to him or her to decide how much to eat at each meal and snack. This will ensure that your child is sensitive to the feelings of fullness and hunger, which will help with weight control in the future. Don't try to force your children to eat everything on their plates when they are clearly not hungry, but make sure that less nutritious foods eaten earlier in the day aren't ruining their appetites. Older children and teenagers usually choose their own snacks, so stock your fridge and pantry with healthy foods. Gradually phasing out less nutritious foods and replacing them with healthier choices is a good way to get children to eat more healthily.

If your child seems to have an endless appetite, look at the types of foods he or she is eating. Foods that are easy to chew and swallow are usually less filling than foods that require some chewing. They can also make it easier to eat more calories. For example, a crunchy apple or pear will take more time to eat than a processed fruit bar or a glass of fruit juice, which also contain more calories. Try gradually replacing less filling foods with more filling versions. For example, substitute wholegrain bread for white bread; lean steak for mince meat; whole fruit for dried fruit, juice and fruit bars; and porridge for cornflakes.

A guide to the minimum number of serves needed from each major food group each day			
	Children 4-7 years	**Children 8-11 years**	**Teenagers 12-18 years**
Bread, rice, pasta, noodles, cereals	2	3	3-4
Vegetables, legumes	2	3	4
Fruit	1	1	2-3
Milk, yoghurt, cheese	2	2	2-2.5
Meat, fish, poultry, eggs, legumes, nuts	0.5	1	1
Adapted from: The Australian guide to healthy eating. Commonwealth Department of Health and Family Services, Canberra, 1998.			

WEIGHT CONTROL FOR CHILDREN

Many children have more body fat than is healthy for them because they eat more calories than they need to fuel their physical activity. Because our lifestyle makes it more difficult to lose weight than gain weight, it's important to try to help prevent children from becoming overweight in the first place. Parents shouldn't dismiss a child's weight problem, believing that he or she will lose their 'puppy fat' with age, nor should they become overly obsessive about weight loss. Ask a doctor or dietitian to determine whether or not your child's weight is healthy.

A healthy diet and regular physical activity will help improve the whole family's health and wellbeing. Regardless of whether or not other family members need to lose weight, weight management for children should be a family affair. Focusing attention on one child's diet and weight can make him or her feel anxious and insecure. Support and encourage your child by feeding the whole family healthy foods as well as being active together, for example by going for a walk in a park or walking your child to school.

WEIGHT CONTROL FOR TEENAGERS

During puberty, rapid physical growth and development means that extra amounts of many nutrients are needed. During a growth spurt, it's normal for teenagers to feel very hungry and eat large amounts of food, but weight gain can occur if their food intake remains high after they've stopped growing, particularly if they're not active.

As with children, weight management for teenagers should be a family affair and should be carefully planned, so that they get all of the nutrients they need for proper development without excess calories. This may require the services of a dietitian, who can also help you and your teenager devise achievable eating strategies for different occasions, and can educate your teenager about healthy food choices.

Some teenagers, particularly females, stop eating red meat or dairy products in an attempt to control their weight. This kind of restrictive eating may not help them lose weight in the long term, and if they don't replace these foods appropriately, they won't be eating enough vitamins, calcium, iron or zinc to meet their increased needs. There are plenty of low-fat dairy products and lean cuts of meat available. Teenagers need to be aware that alcohol, soft drinks, juices and 'junk' foods are more likely to lead to weight gain. Seek help from a doctor and dietitian if your teenager appears to be overly concerned with dieting and their weight.

Another habit among weight-conscious teenagers is skipping meals, particularly breakfast or lunch. This leads to poor concentration and mental performance. Scientific research has shown that this is more likely to result in weight gain because meal skippers tend to overeat later in the day due to excessive hunger. They are also more likely to eat fast food away from home, which can boost their fat and calorie intakes to unhealthy levels.

HELPING AN OVERWEIGHT CHILD OR TEENAGER

1 I Focus on preventing further weight gain, so the child grows into their height. Strict diets and rapid weight loss are not suitable for children.

2 I Keep healthy foods and drinks in the house rather than 'junk' foods.

3 I Serve healthier meals and snacks that are more filling and nutritious.

4 I Don't force children to eat everything on their plate if they aren't hungry.

5 I Use low-fat cooking methods and buy lower-fat foods.

6 I Save soft drinks for special occasions and limit juice or cordial to one glass a day.

7 I Ensure meals and snacks are eaten at the table, not in front of the television.

8 I Reward good behaviour with favourite activities and compliments rather than food.

9 I Make physical activity a priority for the whole family.

10 I Promote healthy foods - explain to your child that healthy foods make you feel healthy and energetic.

BE PREPARED

Keep the fridge and pantry well stocked with healthy foods so you have something nutritious available at all times. Make use of different breads and healthy sandwich fillings, and different types of fruit to give your children a variety of tasty lunches during the week. It's important to give them something that they like, otherwise lunch may end up in the bin or swapped for something less nutritious. If time is an issue in the morning, make lunch in the evening and store it in the fridge overnight.

Healthy snacks for the fridge and pantry

I Fresh, dried and canned fruit
I Carrot and celery sticks
I Bread, English muffins, crumpets, bagels, pikelets, fruit loaf, low-fat crackers and crispbreads
I Baked beans, tinned spaghetti, low-fat instant noodles
I Canned minestrone soup
I Low-fat breakfast cereal bars and ready-to-eat breakfast cereals
I Milk, yoghurt, custard, cheese, low-fat ice cream, frozen fruit juice ice blocks
I Healthy toppings for sandwiches and crackers: boiled eggs, lean ham and other meats, tuna or salmon in water or brine

Healthier fast food choices

I Tetrapak breakfast drinks, smoothies and freshly squeezed juices
I Fruit salad with yoghurt
I Flavoured reduced- or low-fat milk
I Breakfast cereal bars
I Fresh fruit, a small packet of dried fruit, nuts and seeds
I Bread roll, fruit bun or coffee/apple scroll
I Nori rolls, sushi
I Sandwiches and bread rolls with salad and lean meat or chicken
I Pasta with a tomato-based sauce
I Skinless barbecue chicken with corn cobs
I Regular-sized hamburgers without cheese, egg or bacon
I Chinese stir-fried dishes with steamed rice (avoid deep-fried dishes)
I Tostadas, burritos and tacos (not nachos)
I Baked potatoes with low-fat fillings
I Soup with a bread roll

SNACKS ON THE RUN

crumpet with banana & honey

vegetable sticks with cottage cheese

dried fruit snack packs

rice crackers

sushi roll

low-fat breakfast cereal & milk

oven-baked corn chips & salsa

no-fat yoghurt

fruit in natural juice & fruit in jelly

Vita Weat with low-fat cheese & tomato

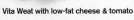
97% fat-free 2-minute noodles

frozen fruit ice blocks

97% fat-free creamed rice pots

pretzels, rice chips & potato chips

fruit muffins & english muffins

fresh fruit

BREAKFAST

spinach & ricotta jaffle

SPINACH & RICOTTA JAFFLE

**8 slices (400 g/13 oz) wholegrain
  bread**
**50 g (1²/₃ oz) baby English
  spinach, finely chopped**
**200 g (6¹/₂ oz) reduced-fat ricotta
  cheese**
**100 g (3¹/₃ oz) semi-dried
  tomatoes**
salt and pepper

1 Preheat a non-stick jaffle maker.
2 Lay 4 slices of the bread on a flat surface.
3 Put the spinach and ricotta into a bowl and mix to combine. Divide the ricotta among the bread slices and top with the semi-dried tomatoes. Season with salt and pepper.
4 Top with the remaining bread slices. Place the sandwiches into the jaffle maker and cook for 3 minutes or until the bread is crunchy and golden on the outside and the filling is warm. Cut into quarters and serve hot. Serves 4
per serve | fat 7 g | protein 13 g | carbohydrate 34.5 g | fibre 5.5 g | cholesterol 21 mg | energy 1065 kJ (255 Cal)

FRUITY FRENCH TOAST

**8 thick slices (400 g/13 oz)
  day-old white hi-fibre bread**
**100 g (3¹/₃ oz) dried apricots,
  chopped**
4 egg whites
**¹/₂ cup (125 ml/4 fl oz) skim or
  no-fat milk**
canola oil spray
2 tablespoons sugar
1 teaspoon cinnamon

1 Lay 4 slices of the bread on a flat surface. Divide the apricots among the bread and press into the center. Top with the remaining bread and press together to seal.
2 Whisk together the egg whites and milk. Dip the bread, one sandwich at a time, into the egg mixture.
3 Lightly spray a non-stick fry pan with canola oil spray and heat over medium heat. Cook the bread until the egg has set and the bread is golden on both sides. Keep the finished sandwiches warm while the remaining sandwiches are cooked.
4 Serve the French toast cut in half and sprinkled with the combined sugar and cinnamon. Serves 4
per serve | fat 3.5 g | protein 13 g | carbohydrate 54.5 g | fibre 6 g | cholesterol 1 mg | energy 1265 kJ (300 Cal)

fruity french toast

dense fruit bread

DENSE FRUIT BREAD

1 Preheat oven to 180°C (350°F/Gas 4). Lightly spray an 18 cm x 11 cm (7 in x 4½ in) loaf tin with canola oil spray and line the base with baking paper.
2 Put the All-Bran and milk into a bowl and set aside for 20 minutes or until the All-Bran is soft.
3 Sift the flour into a bowl. Stir in the sugar, dried fruit salad, figs and All-Bran mixture.
4 Whisk together the egg and margarine, pour into the fruit mixture and mix to combine.
5 Spoon the mixture into the prepared tin, brush the top lightly with water and sprinkle with the poppy seeds. Bake for 1 hour or until the bread starts to come away from the sides of the tin. Allow to cool in the tin for 5 minutes before turning out on a wire rack to cool completely. Slice and spread with canola margarine or jam to serve. Serves 12

per serve I **fat 4.5 g** I **protein 6.5 g** I **carbohydrate 50.5 g** I **fibre 8.5 g** I **cholesterol 16.5 mg** I **energy 1105 kJ (265 Cal)**

canola oil spray
1 cup (65 g/2 oz) All-Bran® (processed wheat bran cereal)
1¼ cups (310 ml/10 fl oz) skim or no-fat milk
2 cups (280 g/9 oz) stone-ground wholemeal self-raising flour
½ cup (115 g/3⅔ oz) firmly packed brown sugar
2 cups (270 g/8⅔ oz) dried fruit salad, roughly chopped
1 cup (210 g/6¾ oz) dried figs, chopped
1 egg, lightly beaten
50 g (1⅔ oz) canola margarine, melted
1 teaspoon poppy seeds

layered brekkie treats

LAYERED BREKKIE TREATS

1 Divide the bananas among 4 wide glasses. Top with half the yoghurt.
2 Divide the muesli among the glasses. Top with the remaining yoghurt.
3 Finish with the berries and drizzle with the maple syrup. Serves 4

per serve | fat 2.5 g | protein 8.5 g | carbohydrate 44.5 g | fibre 4.5 g | cholesterol 10 mg | energy 1005 kJ (240 Cal)

2 medium bananas, sliced
400 g (13 oz) reduced-fat Greek-style plain yoghurt
1 cup (100 g/3$\frac{1}{3}$ oz) low-fat natural muesli
200 g (6$\frac{1}{2}$ oz) mixed fresh or frozen berries
2 tablespoons maple syrup

BAKED BEANS IN BREAD CUPS

1 Preheat oven to 200°C (400°F/Gas 6). Lightly spray a 4 x 1 cup (250 ml/8 fl oz) capacity non-stick muffin pan with canola oil spray.
2 Line the base of each muffin hole with a slice of bread. Divide a third of the beans among the muffin holes, then top with a third of the cheese. Repeat the layers and finish with a layer of bread.
3 Whisk together the egg, egg whites and milk. Slowly pour the egg mixture into each muffin hole. Set aside for 10 minutes or until the egg mixture has been absorbed. Top with the remaining beans and cheese.
4 Bake for 35 minutes or until the bread is crisp and golden. Serves 4

per serve | fat 5.5 g | protein 18.5 g | carbohydrate 46 g | fibre 8.5 g | cholesterol 52.5 mg | energy 1295 kJ (310 Cal)

canola oil spray
12 slices (600 g/1 lb 3 oz) wholegrain bread, crusts removed
400 g (13 oz) can reduced-salt baked beans
$\frac{1}{4}$ cup (30 g/1 oz) grated reduced-fat cheddar cheese
1 egg, lightly beaten
2 egg whites, lightly beaten
$\frac{1}{2}$ cup (125 ml/4 fl oz) skim or no-fat milk

baked beans in bread cups

fruity couscous

FRUITY COUSCOUS

1¹/₂ cups (375 ml/12 fl oz)
   unsweetened orange juice
1 cinnamon stick
1 cup (185 g/6 oz) couscous
1 medium peach, chopped
1 medium plum, chopped
1 medium nectarine, chopped
1 medium mango, chopped
200 g (6¹/₂ oz) no-fat, no-added
   sugar peach and mango yoghurt
2 tablespoons golden syrup

1 Put the orange juice and cinnamon stick into a pan and bring to the boil. Pour over the couscous and set aside for 10 minutes or until the liquid has been absorbed.

2 Separate the couscous grains with a fork. Add the fruit and mix gently to combine.

3 Serve in bowls topped with the yoghurt and golden syrup. Serves 6

per serve | fat 0.5 g | protein 7 g | carbohydrate 46 g | fibre 2 g | cholesterol 1.5 mg | energy 915 kJ (220 Cal)

BANANA & BLUEBERRY PANCAKES

2 cups (250 g/8 oz) self-raising
   flour
¹/₄ cup (60 g/2 oz) firmly packed
   brown sugar
4 egg whites, lightly beaten
¹/₂ cup (125 ml/4 fl oz) skim or
   no-fat milk
200 g (6¹/₂ oz) no-fat, no-added
   sugar vanilla yoghurt
2 cups (480 g/15 oz) mashed
   banana
150 g (5 oz) blueberries
canola oil spray

1 Sift the flour into a large bowl and stir in the sugar. Whisk together the egg whites, milk and yoghurt. Stir into the dry ingredients.

2 Add the banana and blueberries and stir until the batter is smooth. Leave for 10 minutes.

3 Lightly spray a non-stick fry pan with canola oil spray. Pour ¹/₄ cup (60 ml/2 fl oz) of the batter into the pan and cook over medium heat until bubbles appear on the surface.

4 Turn the pancake over and cook the other side until browned. Keep warm while you cook the remaining batter. Serve drizzled with maple syrup. Makes 12

per pancake | fat 0.5 g | protein 5.5 g | carbohydrate 30.5 g | fibre 2 g | cholesterol 1.5 mg | energy 625 kJ (150 Cal)

banana & blueberry pancakes

hash browns with tomatoes & mushrooms

HASH BROWNS WITH TOMATOES & MUSHROOMS

1 Cook the potatoes in a large pan of boiling water for 10 minutes or until just tender. Drain and leave to cool.

2 Grate the potatoes into a bowl. Season with salt and pepper. Shape the mixture into 8 flat patties and place onto a baking tray lined with baking paper.

3 Arrange the tomatoes and mushrooms on a baking tray, drizzle with half the balsamic vinegar and place under a grill preheated to high. Cook for 5 minutes or until soft. Turn the mushrooms, drizzle with the remaining balsamic vinegar and cook for 10 minutes or until browned. Remove the tomatoes and mushrooms from the grill and keep warm.

4 Lightly spray the patties with olive oil spray. Place under a grill preheated to high and cook for 5-10 minutes or until crisp and golden. Turn over, lightly spray with olive oil spray and cook the other side. Serve with the tomatoes and mushrooms.

Serves 4

per serve I **fat 1 g** I **protein 4.5 g** I **carbohydrate 16.5 g** I **fibre 3.5 g** I **cholesterol 0 mg** I **energy 415 kJ (100 Cal)**

500 g (1 lb) potatoes, unpeeled and halved
salt and pepper
4 Roma tomatoes, halved
8 (700 g/1 lb 6½ oz) field mushrooms
2 tablespoons balsamic vinegar
olive oil spray

BERRY DELICIOUS MUFFINS

4 (60 g/2 oz) breakfast wheat
   biscuits, crushed
3/4 cup (185 ml/6 fl oz) skim or
   no-fat milk
1 1/2 cups (210 g/6 3/4 oz)
   wholemeal self-raising flour
3 tablespoons brown sugar
4 egg whites
1 tablespoon canola oil
140 ml (4 1/2 fl oz) apple and
   raspberry puree
200 g (6 1/2 oz) mixed fresh or
   frozen berries
2 tablespoons fruits of the forest
   no-added sugar fruit spread

1 Preheat oven to 180°C (350°F/Gas 4). Line an 8 x 1/3 cup (80 ml/2 2/3 fl oz) capacity non-stick muffin pan with muffin cases.

2 Put the wheat biscuits and milk into a bowl and set aside for 10 minutes or until the biscuits are soft.

3 Sift the flour into a bowl, stir in the sugar and make a well in the center. Whisk together the egg whites, canola oil and apple and raspberry puree, pour into the well along with the wheat biscuit mixture and mix until just combined. Fold through three-quarters of the mixed berries.

4 Half-fill each muffin hole with the batter, top with 1 teaspoon of the fruit spread, then top with the remaining batter. Press the remaining berries into the top of each muffin.

5 Bake for 30 minutes or until the muffins are golden and start to come away from the side of the pan. Allow to cool for 5 minutes before turning out on a wire rack to cool. Makes 8

per muffin | fat 3 g | protein 7 g | carbohydrate 31 g | fibre 4.5 g | cholesterol 0.5 mg | energy 760 kJ (180 Cal)

berry delicious muffins

ham, egg & tomato wrap

HAM, EGG & TOMATO WRAP

1 Whisk together the eggs, egg whites and parsley. Season with salt and pepper.

2 Lightly spray a non-stick fry pan with canola oil spray and heat over medium heat. Add the egg mixture to the pan and cook until it just starts to set. Stir until the mixture is lightly scrambled. Cook for 2 minutes.

3 Lay the lavash or mountain bread on a flat surface. Divide the ham among the bread and place it along one edge. Top the ham with the egg, tomatoes and spinach. Gently roll up in greaseproof paper to enclose the filling. Cut in half and serve hot or cold. Serves 4

per serve | fat 5.5 g | protein 16.5 g | carbohydrate 34.5 g | fibre 6 g | cholesterol 106.5 mg | energy 1065 kJ (255 Cal)

2 eggs, lightly beaten

2 egg whites, lightly beaten

1 tablespoon chopped fresh parsley

salt and pepper

canola oil spray

4 slices (215 g/7 oz) wholemeal lavash or mountain bread

100 g (3¹/₃ oz) shaved 97% fat-free honey ham

2 medium tomatoes, thinly sliced

50 g (1²/₃ oz) baby English spinach

DRINKS & SNACKS

my mum's little date loaves

MY MUM'S LITTLE DATE LOAVES

1 cup (190 g/6¼ oz) pitted dates
1 cup (250 ml/8 fl oz) water
1 teaspoon bicarbonate of soda
  (baking soda)
1 tablespoon reduced-fat canola
  margarine
1 cup (250 g/8 oz) caster sugar
2 cups (250 g/8 oz) self-raising
  flour
1 egg, lightly beaten

1 Preheat oven to 180°C (350°F/Gas 4). Lightly grease 8 x ½ cup (125 ml/4 fl oz) capacity mini loaf tins and line the bases with baking paper.
2 Put the dates and water into a pan. Bring to the boil, then reduce the heat and simmer for 5 minutes. Cool slightly, then stir in the bicarbonate of soda and margarine. Transfer to a bowl.
3 Add the sugar, sifted flour and egg and mix to combine. Spoon the mixture into the tins. Bake for 20 minutes or until a skewer comes out clean when inserted into the center. Serve with reduced-fat margarine, fruit spread or yoghurt. Makes 8
per loaf I fat 2 g I protein 4.5 g I carbohydrate 64 g I fibre 3.5 g I cholesterol 23.5 mg I energy 1205 kJ (290 Cal)

CRUNCHY LOW-FAT ICED CHOCOLATE

⅓ cup (80 ml/2⅔ fl oz)
  chocolate topping
3 cups (750 ml/24 fl oz) low-fat
  chocolate milk
4 large scoops (160 g/5⅓ oz)
  low-fat vanilla ice cream
4 tablespoons Milo® drink powder

1 Swirl the chocolate topping around the inside of 4 tall glasses and freeze until set.
2 Divide the chocolate milk among the glasses. Carefully drop a scoop of ice cream into each glass. Top with the Milo and serve immediately. Serves 4
per serve I fat 3 g I protein 12.5 g I carbohydrate 39.5 g I fibre 0 g I cholesterol 14 mg I energy 960 kJ (230 Cal)

crunchy low-fat iced chocolate

up & at 'em powershakes

UP & AT 'EM POWERSHAKES

1 To make either banana malt powershakes or mango raspberry powershakes, put the chopped fruit into a blender.

2 Add the remaining ingredients. Blend until thick and creamy. Pour into 4 tall glasses and sprinkle with nutmeg. Serves 4

per serve (banana malt) | fat 1.5 g | protein 10.5 g | carbohydrate 27.5 g | fibre 3 g | cholesterol 1.5 mg | energy 690 kJ (165 Cal)

per serve (mango raspberry) | fat 1.5 g | protein 10 g | carbohydrate 23.5 g | fibre 4 g | cholesterol 1.5 mg | energy 625 kJ (150 Cal)

BANANA MALT

2 medium bananas, chopped

1 (15 g/$^1/_2$ oz) breakfast wheat biscuit, crushed

2 tablespoons wheatgerm

2 tablespoons malted milk powder or skim milk powder

2 tablespoons no-fat, no-added sugar honey yoghurt

3 cups (750 ml/24 fl oz) low-fat vanilla soy milk, chilled

ground nutmeg, to serve

MANGO RASPBERRY

1 (210 g/6$^3/_4$ oz) mango, sliced

125 g (4 oz) raspberries, halved

2 tablespoons wheatgerm

2 tablespoons malted milk powder or skim milk powder

2 tablespoons no-fat, no-added sugar honey yoghurt

3 cups (750 ml/24 fl oz) low-fat vanilla soy milk, chilled

ground nutmeg, to serve

miso noodle soup

MISO NOODLE SOUP

1 Put the miso, dashi and water into a pan and stir until the miso dissolves. Cook over medium heat until the miso is hot; do not let the mixture boil.
2 Add the noodles to the pan and cook over medium heat until heated through.
3 Serve the soup sprinkled with the spring onions and tofu. Serves 4 as a snack

per serve | fat 4.5 g | protein 9.5 g | carbohydrate 16 g | fibre 2.5 g | cholesterol 0 mg | energy 580 kJ (140 Cal)

2 tablespoons white miso paste
1 teaspoon dashi granules
4 cups (1 litre/32 fl oz) water
200 g (6$\frac{1}{2}$ oz) fresh udon noodles
2 spring onions (scallions), sliced
200 g (6$\frac{1}{2}$ oz) soft tofu, diced

NOT-SO-NAUGHTY WEDGES

1 Preheat oven to 220°C (425°F/Gas 7).
2 Put the potato and sweet potato into a large baking dish, lightly spray with olive oil spray and sprinkle with sea salt. Bake for 45 minutes or until the wedges are crisp and golden.
3 Serve the wedges with the combined yoghurt and sweet chilli sauce. Serves 6 as a snack

per serve | fat 2 g | protein 5 g | carbohydrate 27 g | fibre 3.5 g | cholesterol 2 mg | energy 610 kJ (145 Cal)

500 g (1 lb) unpeeled potatoes, cut into wedges
500 g (1 lb) unpeeled orange sweet potato, cut into wedges
olive oil spray
sea salt
$\frac{1}{2}$ cup (125 g/4 oz) reduced-fat Greek-style plain yoghurt
$\frac{1}{4}$ cup (60 ml/2 fl oz) sweet chilli sauce or tomato sauce

not-so-naughty wedges

swirly whirly meringues

SWIRLY WHIRLY MERINGUES

3 egg whites
¾ cup (180 g/6 oz) caster sugar
1 teaspoon cornflour
1 teaspoon white vinegar
red food colouring

1 Preheat oven to 120°C (250°F/Gas ½). Line 2 baking trays with baking paper.

2 Whisk the egg whites in a clean, dry bowl until stiff peaks form. Add the sugar, 1 tablespoon at a time, until the mixture is stiff and glossy.

3 Fold the cornflour and vinegar through the meringue mixture. Drop heaped spoonfuls of the meringue onto the trays. Use a wooden skewer to swirl the colouring through the meringues.

4 Bake for 40 minutes or until crisp. Turn off the oven and allow the meringues to cool in the oven. Serve with fresh fruit and low-fat yoghurt for dipping. Makes 12

per meringue | fat 0 g | protein 1 g | carbohydrate 15 g | fibre 0 g | cholesterol 0 mg | energy 260 kJ (60 Cal)

CHEESE & HERB POPCORN

½ cup (95 g/3 oz) natural flavour microwave popcorn
20 g (¾ oz) reduced-fat canola margarine
1 tablespoon chopped fresh herbs (parsley, chives)
2 tablespoons finely grated parmesan cheese

1 Cook the popcorn according to the manufacturer's instructions. Transfer to a large bowl.

2 Put the margarine and herbs into a pan and cook over low heat until the margarine has melted.

3 Pour the herb mixture over the popcorn, sprinkle with the parmesan cheese and toss to combine. Serves 8 as a snack

per serve | fat 7 g | protein 1.5 g | carbohydrate 4 g | fibre 1.5 g | cholesterol 1.5 mg | energy 350 kJ (85 Cal)

cheese & herb popcorn

bean, cheese & tomato quesadillas

BEAN, CHEESE & TOMATO QUESADILLAS

1 Lay 4 of the tortillas on a flat surface. Spread the beans over the tortillas, leaving a 1 cm (½ in) border. Top with the tomatoes, jalepeño peppers, cheese and remaining tortillas.

2 Lightly spray a non-stick fry pan with canola oil spray. Add a tortilla and weigh it down with a plate. Cook over medium heat for 2 minutes or until the bottom tortilla is crisp and golden.

3 Slide the tortilla out of the pan and onto a plate. Return to the pan and cook the other side until crisp and golden. Repeat with the remaining tortillas. Cut into wedges to serve. Serves 6 as a snack

per serve | fat 4.5 g | protein 8 g | carbohydrate 19 g | fibre 3 g | cholesterol 6 mg | energy 615 kJ (145 Cal)

8 medium flour tortillas, 15 cm
    (6 in) diameter
200 g (6½ oz) can refried beans
2 medium tomatoes, thinly sliced
1 tablespoon chopped bottled
    jalapeño peppers (optional)
½ cup (60 g/2 oz) grated
    reduced-fat cheddar cheese
canola oil spray

RED BERRY SLUSHIES

1 Put the berries into a blender.

2 Add the frozen fruit dessert, raspberry cranberry juice and ice. Blend until thick and slushy. If the slushie is too thick, add a little extra juice. Serves 8

per serve | fat 0 g | protein 0.5 g | carbohydrate 16.5 g | fibre 0.5 g | cholesterol 0 mg | energy 295 kJ (70 Cal)

250 g (8 oz) mixed fresh or frozen
    berries
2 cups (320 g/10⅔ oz) berry
    fat-free frozen fruit dessert
2 cups (500 ml/16 fl oz) raspberry
    cranberry juice
2 cups (270 g/8⅔ oz) ice

red berry slushies

nachos

NACHOS

400 g (13 oz) can refried beans
200 g (6 1/2 oz) mild tomato salsa
1/2 small Lebanese cucumber,
    unpeeled and diced
225 g (7 oz) oven-baked corn
    chips
1/3 cup (40 g/1 1/3 oz) grated
    reduced-fat cheddar cheese
200 g (6 1/2 oz) reduced-fat
    Greek-style plain yoghurt

1 Preheat oven to 200°C (400°F/Gas 6).
2 Put the refried beans and 2 tablespoons of the tomato salsa into a bowl and mix to combine. Combine the cucumber with the remaining salsa and set aside.
3 Spread the bean mixture onto the center of a heatproof shallow plate. Arrange the corn chips in the beans.
4 Sprinkle with the grated cheese* and bake for 5-10 minutes or until the cheese is bubbling and golden. Serve with the yoghurt and the cucumber and salsa mixture. Serves 8 as a snack
per serve | fat 3 g | protein 9 g | carbohydrate 33 g | fibre 4 g | cholesterol 5.5 mg | energy 825 kJ (195 Cal)
* Add 2 teaspoons chopped bottled jalapeños with the cheese for a spicy flavour.

APPLE BERRY JELLIES

2 cups (500 ml/16 fl oz)
    unsweetened apple juice
1 tablespoon gelatin
150 g (5 oz) mixed fresh berries

1 Line a 12 x 1/3 cup (80 ml/2 2/3 fl oz) capacity muffin pan with a double layer of small muffin cases.
2 Put the apple juice and gelatin into a pan and stir over low heat until the gelatin dissolves. Set aside to cool slightly.
3 Divide the berries among the muffin holes. Half-fill the holes with the apple juice mixture and refrigerate until set. Top with the remaining juice mixture and refrigerate until set. Makes 12
per jelly | fat 0 g | protein 1 g | carbohydrate 5 g | fibre 0.3 g | cholesterol 0 mg | energy 100 kJ (25 Cal)

apple berry jellies

bubble snack bar

BUBBLE SNACK BAR

1 Lightly grease a 25 cm x 17 cm (10 in x 6¾ in) tin and line with baking paper.
2 Put the puffed rice, muesli, apricots, pepitas, sunflower seeds and sesame seeds into a bowl and mix to combine.
3 Put the malted rice syrup and marshmallows into a pan and stir over low heat until the marshmallows have melted.
4 Pour the syrup mixture into the puffed rice mixture and mix to combine. Press into the tin and refrigerate for 2-3 hours or until set. Cut into 20 squares. The bars will soften at room temperature, so keep refrigerated. Makes 20

per bar I fat 3 g I protein 2.5 g I carbohydrate 17.5 g I fibre 1.5 g I cholesterol < 0.1 mg I energy 430 kJ **(100 Cal)**

* Malted rice syrup is available from health-food shops.

2 cups (60 g/2 oz) puffed rice cereal
1½ cups (150 g/5 oz) natural muesli
100 g (3⅓ oz) dried apricots, chopped
¼ cup (40 g/1⅓ oz) pepitas
¼ cup (30 g/1 oz) sunflower seeds
2 tablespoons sesame seeds
⅓ cup (80 ml/2⅔ fl oz) malted rice syrup* or honey
100 g (3⅓ oz) white marshmallows

mmm hot choccy

MMM HOT CHOCCY

1 Put the milk, Milo and malted milk powder into a pan and stir over low heat until the Milo is dissolved. Increase the heat and cook until the milk is just about to boil.

2 Divide the mixture among 4 mugs. Top each mug with 3 marshmallows. Serves 4

per serve | fat 1.5 g | protein 11.5 g | carbohydrate 30.5 g | fibre 0 g | cholesterol 10.6 mg | energy 715 kJ (170 Cal)

4 cups (1 litre/32 fl oz) reduced-fat milk
4 tablespoons Milo® drink powder
4 tablespoons malted milk powder
12 white marshmallows

CREAMY CORN HUMMUS WITH PITA CHIPS

1 Cut the pita bread in half through the center, then into large triangles. Spray lightly with olive oil spray and sprinkle with the parmesan cheese. Arrange on 2 non-stick baking trays and place under a grill preheated to high. Cook until crisp and golden on both sides.

2 Put the chickpeas, garlic, tahini, lemon juice and creamed corn into a food processor. Process until thick and creamy.

3 Serve pots of the creamy corn hummus with the pita chips and carrot, celery, asparagus and bean sticks. Serves 10 as a snack

per serve | fat 5 g | protein 6 g | carbohydrate 22.5 g | fibre 4 g | cholesterol 2 mg | energy 660 kJ (160 Cal)

3 medium (225 g/7 oz) pita bread
olive oil spray
1/4 cup (25 g/1 oz) finely grated parmesan cheese
400 g (13 oz) can chickpeas, rinsed and drained
1 clove garlic
2 tablespoons tahini
1/4 cup (60 ml/2 fl oz) lemon juice
400 g (13 oz) can creamed corn

creamy corn hummus with pita chips

jungle punch

JUNGLE PUNCH

¹/₄ cup fresh mint leaves
250 g (8 oz) strawberries
2 cups (500 ml/16 fl oz) tropical
   fruit juice
3 cups (750 ml/24 fl oz) sparkling
   apple juice
2 cups (500 ml/16 fl oz) pineapple
   juice
300 g (10 oz) peeled pineapple,
   chopped

1 Put the mint leaves into ice cube holes, cover with water and freeze until firm. Halve the strawberries and freeze until firm.
2 Put the tropical fruit juice, sparkling apple juice and pineapple juice into a large punch bowl or jug. Add the mint ice cubes, frozen strawberries and pineapple. Serve immediately. Serves 10
per serve | fat 0.5 g | protein 1.5 g | carbohydrate 22 g | fibre 3 g | cholesterol 0 mg | energy 410 kJ (100 Cal)

YOGHURT BERRY ICE POPS

400 g (13 oz) mixed fresh or
   frozen berries
200 g (6¹/₂ oz) no-fat, no-added
   sugar honey yoghurt
50 g (1²/₃ oz) white chocolate,
   roughly chopped (optional)

1 Put the berries, yoghurt and white chocolate (if using) into a bowl and mix to combine, crushing the berries slightly to release some of the colour into the yoghurt. Divide the mixture among 8 x ¹/₂ cup (125 ml/4 fl oz) capacity ice block moulds. Add the sticks and freeze until firm.
2 Rub a warm cloth over the outside of each ice block hole and gently pull the stick to remove. Makes 8
per ice pop (with chocolate) | fat 2 g | protein 2.5 g | carbohydrate 6.5 g | fibre 1 g | cholesterol 3.5 mg | energy 235 kJ (55 Cal)
per ice pop (without chocolate) | fat 0 g | protein 2 g | carbohydrate 3 g | fibre 1 g | cholesterol 2 mg | energy 95 kJ (25 Cal)

yoghurt berry ice pops

LUNCH BOXES

bbq chicken wrap

BBQ CHICKEN WRAP

4 (110 g/3½ oz) Lebanese bread
   rounds
2 tablespoons tomato chutney
2 tablespoons low-fat mayonnaise
2 cups (300 g/10 oz) finely
   shredded barbecue chicken
   (white meat only)
1 cup (115 g/3⅔ oz) grated carrot
1 medium Lebanese cucumber,
   unpeeled and thinly sliced
50 g (1⅔ oz) baby English
   spinach

1 Lay the Lebanese bread on a flat surface. Spread the tomato chutney along one edge and top with the mayonnaise.
2 Divide the chicken among the bread and top with the carrot, cucumber and spinach. Roll up in plastic wrap to enclose the filling and twist the ends to seal.
3 Cut in half and serve. Makes 4 (Serves 8)

per wrap | fat 9 g | protein 29.5 g | carbohydrate 54 g | fibre 4.5 g | cholesterol 69.5 mg | energy 1750 kJ (420 Cal)

per serve | fat 4.5 g | protein 14.5 g | carbohydrate 27 g | fibre 2 g | cholesterol 35 mg | energy 875 kJ (210 Cal)

THAI NOODLE SALAD

400 g (13 oz) fresh Hokkien
   noodles
250 g (8 oz) asparagus, chopped
225 g (7 oz) broccoli florets
3 spring onions (scallions), sliced
1 medium carrot, thinly sliced
1 medium red capsicum (bell
   pepper), thinly sliced
2 cups (150 g/5 oz) shredded
   Chinese cabbage
2 tablespoons sweet chilli sauce
1 tablespoon lime juice
1 tablespoon fish sauce

1 Separate the noodles, put into a bowl, cover with boiling water and stand for 2 minutes or until just soft. Drain well.
2 Boil or steam the asparagus and broccoli until bright green and tender. Drain well.
3 Put the noodles, asparagus, broccoli, spring onions, carrot, capsicum and cabbage into a bowl and mix to combine.
4 Whisk together the chilli sauce, lime juice and fish sauce. Pour over the salad and toss to combine. Serve in take-away Chinese boxes. Serves 6

per serve | fat 4.5 g | protein 6.5 g | carbohydrate 18 g | fibre 5.5 g | cholesterol 1.5 mg | energy 590 kJ (140 Cal)

thai noodle salad

pumpkin & pasta cups

PUMPKIN & PASTA CUPS

1 Preheat oven to 180°C (350°F/Gas 4). Lightly spray a 6 x 1 cup (250 ml/8 fl oz) capacity non-stick muffin pan with canola oil spray.
2 Cook the pasta in a large pan of rapidly boiling water until al dente (cooked, but still with a bite to it). Drain well and transfer to a large bowl.
3 Add the pumpkin, capsicum, parsley and fetta to the pasta and mix to combine. Season with salt and pepper. Divide the mixture among the muffin holes.
4 Whisk together the eggs, egg whites, milk and cheese. Pour over the pasta mixture. Bake for 35 minutes or until the egg is set and starts to come away from the side of the pan. Makes 6

per pasta cup | fat 6 g | protein 16.5 g | carbohydrate 30 g | fibre 2.5 g | cholesterol 80 mg | energy 1000 kJ (240 Cal)

canola oil spray
200 g (6$\frac{1}{2}$ oz) spiral pasta
300 g (10 oz) cooked chopped pumpkin (roasted or boiled)
100 g (3$\frac{1}{3}$ oz) chargrilled red capsicum (bell pepper), cut into thick strips
2 tablespoons roughly chopped fresh flat-leaf parsley
50 g (1$\frac{2}{3}$ oz) reduced-fat fetta cheese, broken into bite-size pieces
salt and pepper
2 eggs, lightly beaten
3 egg whites
$\frac{1}{2}$ cup (125 ml/4 fl oz) skim or no-fat milk
$\frac{1}{3}$ cup (40 g/1$\frac{1}{3}$ oz) grated reduced-fat cheddar cheese

ham & cheese super sandwich

HAM & CHEESE SUPER SANDWICH

1 Cut the bread into 4 x 10 cm (4 in) pieces. Cut each piece in half through the center.

2 Lay the bread bases on a flat surface and spread with the mustard. Top with the sprouts, tomatoes, cheese, cucumbers and ham. Replace the bread tops. Serves 4

per serve | fat 9 g | protein 28 g | carbohydrate 77.5 g | fibre 3.5 g | cholesterol 30 mg | energy 2005 kJ (480 Cal)

1 loaf (620 g/1$^1/_4$ lb) wholemeal Turkish bread
2 tablespoons wholegrain honey mustard
50 g (1$^2/_3$ oz) alfalfa sprouts
2 medium tomatoes, sliced
100 g (3$^1/_3$ oz) shaved reduced-fat Swiss cheese
$^1/_3$ cup (50 g/1$^2/_3$ oz) sliced bread and butter cucumbers
100 g (3$^1/_3$ oz) shaved 97% fat-free honey ham

CORN COBS WITH TUNA FINGERS

1 Cut the corn cobs in half. Cook in a large pan of boiling water until tender, then drain. Lightly spray the corn with olive oil spray, roll in the chives and sprinkle with the sea salt.

2 Put the tuna, spring onions, celery, mayonnaise and lemon juice into a bowl and mix to combine.

3 Lay 4 slices of the bread on a flat surface. Divide the tuna mixture among the bread, top with the remaining bread slices and cut each sandwich into 3 fingers. Serve with the corn cobs. Serves 4

per serve | fat 7 g | protein 26.5 g | carbohydrate 40.5 g | fibre 7 g | cholesterol 40.5 mg | energy 1400 kJ (335 Cal)

2 large cobs sweet corn
olive oil spray
1 tablespoon chopped fresh chives
sea salt
400 g (13 oz) can tuna in brine, drained
2 spring onions (scallions), sliced
1 celery stick, thinly sliced
3 tablespoons low-fat mayonnaise
1 teaspoon lemon juice
8 thick slices (320 g/10$^2/_3$ oz) white hi-fibre bread, crusts removed

corn cobs with tuna fingers

marinated vegetable & beef cobs

MARINATED VEGETABLE & BEEF COBS

4 small (120 g/4 oz) wholegrain
  bread rolls
100 g (3¹/₃ oz) reduced-fat
  creamed cottage cheese
50 g (1²/₃ oz) baby English
  spinach
150 g (5 oz) chargrilled red
  capsicum (bell pepper),
  cut into thick strips
100 g (3¹/₃ oz) chargrilled
  mushrooms
4 hard-boiled eggs, sliced
100 g (3¹/₃ oz) shaved lean
  roast beef

1 Cut off and reserve the tops of the bread rolls.
Pull out the center of the rolls, leaving a 1 cm (½ in)
bread crust.
2 Spoon the cottage cheese into each bread roll and
top with the spinach, pressing down firmly. Follow
with the red capsicum, mushrooms, eggs and beef,
packing each layer firmly.
3 Replace the tops of the bread rolls, wrap each roll
firmly with plastic wrap and refrigerate overnight.
4 Cut the rolls in half and serve. Serves 4
per serve I fat 9 g I protein 22 g I carbohydrate 18.5 g
I fibre 3.5 g I cholesterol 236.5 mg I energy 1020 kJ
(245 Cal)

BAKED RICOTTA WEDGES WITH GREEK SALAD

400 g (13 oz) wedge reduced-fat
  ricotta cheese
1 tablespoon lemon zest
2 tablespoons chopped fresh
  flat-leaf parsley
olive oil spray
½ teaspoon sweet paprika
1 small red capsicum (bell
  pepper), chopped
1 medium Lebanese cucumber,
  unpeeled and thickly sliced
200 g (6½ oz) grape tomatoes,
  halved
8 kalamata olives in brine, drained
  and pitted
¼ cup (60 ml/2 fl oz) fat-free
  Italian salad dressing

1 Preheat oven to 220°C (425°F/Gas 7).
2 Cut the ricotta into 4 wedges and place onto a
non-stick baking tray. Put the lemon zest and
parsley into a bowl and mix to combine. Press onto
the top and side of the ricotta, lightly spray with
olive oil spray and sprinkle with the paprika. Bake
for 20 minutes or until golden brown.
3 Put the capsicum, cucumber, tomatoes and olives
into a bowl and mix gently to combine.
4 Serve the ricotta wedges with the salad, dressing
and toasted Turkish bread to the side. Serves 4
per serve I fat 11.5 g I protein 14 g I carbohydrate
10.5 g I fibre 2 g I cholesterol 52.5 mg I energy 840 kJ
(200 Cal)

baked ricotta wedges with greek salad

sushi in a bowl

SUSHI IN A BOWL

1 Whisk together the egg and egg yolk. Lightly spray a non-stick fry pan with canola oil spray and heat over medium heat. Pour in the egg mixture, cook until the egg has set, turn over and cook the other side. Remove from the pan and cool slightly. Finely shred the egg.

2 Put the rice and water into a pan and bring to the boil. Cook over high heat until tunnels appear in the rice. Reduce the heat, cover and cook over very low heat for 15 minutes or until the rice is tender. Add the rice vinegar and mix to combine. Transfer to a bowl, cover and leave to cool.

3 Put the tuna, mayonnaise and spring onion into a bowl and mix to combine.

4 Divide the rice among 4 bowls. Top with the nori sheets, cucumber, carrot, shredded egg and tuna mixture. Serves 4

per serve I fat 5.5 g I protein 15 g I carbohydrate 47 g I fibre 4 g I cholesterol 110.5 mg I energy 1250 kJ (300 Cal)

1 egg

1 egg yolk

canola oil spray

1 cup (220 g/7 oz) Japanese sushi rice

3 cups (750 ml/24 fl oz) water

1 tablespoon seasoned rice vinegar

180 g (6 oz) can tuna in spring water, drained

1 tablespoon low-fat mayonnaise

1 spring onion (scallion), thinly sliced

4 sheets (20 g/¾ oz) nori seaweed, sliced

1 medium Lebanese cucumber, unpeeled and sliced

1 medium carrot, grated

chicken noodle balls

CHICKEN NOODLE BALLS

1 Preheat oven to 220°C (425°F/Gas 7).
2 Separate the noodles, put into a bowl, cover with boiling water and stand for 2 minutes or until tender. Drain well and cut into short lengths using scissors.
3 Put the noodles, chicken, onion, breadcrumbs, spices, chilli sauce and coriander into a bowl and mix well to combine.
4 Shape heaped tablespoons of the mixture into balls and place on 2 non-stick baking trays. Lightly spray with canola oil spray and bake for 25 minutes or until golden and tender. Serve with tomato sauce and sweet chilli sauce for dipping. Makes 16

per noodle ball | fat 3 g | protein 6.5 g | carbohydrate 4.5 g | fibre 0.5 g | cholesterol 15 mg | energy 295 kJ (70 Cal)

200 g (6^1/$_2$ oz) fresh Hokkien
   noodles
500 g (1 lb) lean chicken mince
1 medium onion, grated
1 cup (70 g/2^1/$_4$ oz) fresh
   breadcrumbs
1 teaspoon ground coriander
1 teaspoon ground cumin
2 tablespoons sweet chilli sauce
2 tablespoons chopped fresh
   coriander (cilantro)
canola oil spray

EASY SAN CHOY BOW

1 Heat the oil in a wok, add the spring onions and cook over high heat until soft. Add the pork mince and cook over high heat until browned.
2 Add the water chestnuts and noodles and stir fry until the noodles are soft.
3 Stir in the stock and oyster sauce and cook until heated through.
4 Serve the pork mixture in lunch boxes with the lettuce leaves and a piece of tropical fruit. Serves 4

per serve | fat 10 g | protein 23 g | carbohydrate 18 g | fibre 2 g | cholesterol 60 mg | energy 1060 kJ (255 Cal)

2 teaspoons canola oil
3 spring onions (scallions), sliced
400 g (13 oz) lean pork mince
200 g (6^1/$_2$ oz) can water
   chestnuts, drained and chopped
200 g (6^1/$_2$ oz) fresh udon
   noodles, separated
2 tablespoons reduced-salt
   chicken stock
2 tablespoons oyster sauce
8 small iceberg lettuce leaves

easy san choy bow

rainbow couscous & salmon salad

RAINBOW COUSCOUS & SALMON SALAD

1 cup (185 g/6 oz) couscous

1¹/₂ cups (375 ml/12 fl oz) boiling
water

1 medium carrot, sliced

200 g (6¹/₂ oz) trimmed green
beans

1 medium red (Spanish) onion,
thinly sliced

300 g (10 oz) can chickpeas,
rinsed and drained

350 g (12 oz) chargrilled
vegetables, such as mushrooms,
zucchini (courgette), capsicum
(bell pepper)

300 g (10 oz) can red salmon in
brine or water, drained

¹/₄ cup (60 ml/2 fl oz) fat-free
Italian salad dressing

1 Put the couscous into a bowl, pour over the boiling water and set aside for 10 minutes or until the liquid has been absorbed. Separate the couscous grains with a fork.

2 Boil or steam the carrot and beans until tender, then drain well.

3 Add the carrot, beans, onion, chickpeas, chargrilled vegetables and salmon to the couscous. Pour over the dressing and mix gently to combine. Serve with baby cos lettuce leaves and a crunchy bread roll. Serves 6

per serve | fat 5.5 g | protein 16.5 g | carbohydrate 33.5 g | fibre 4.5 g | cholesterol 25.5 mg | energy 1050 kJ (250 Cal)

ASIAN RICE BALLS

2¹/₂ cups (430 g/15 oz) cooked
Japanese sushi rice

3 spring onions (scallions), thinly
sliced

1 celery stick, sliced

1 medium carrot, finely grated

1 egg white, lightly beaten

2 tablespoons sesame seeds

1 tablespoon reduced-salt soy
sauce

canola oil spray

1 Preheat oven to 220°C (425°F/Gas 7). Line a baking tray with baking paper.

2 Put the cooled rice, spring onions, celery, carrot, egg white, sesame seeds and soy sauce into a bowl and mix well to combine.

3 Shape the mixture into 6 balls. Arrange the balls on the prepared tray. Lightly spray with canola oil spray and bake for 20 minutes or until crisp and golden. Serve with plum sauce for dipping and a crisp garden salad. Makes 6

per rice ball | fat 2.5 g | protein 3.5 g | carbohydrate 21 g | fibre 1.5 g | cholesterol 0 mg | energy 520 kJ (125 Cal)

asian rice balls

chunky tater & pea salad

CHUNKY TATER & PEA SALAD

1 Cook the potatoes in a large pan of boiling water until just tender. Add the peas and cook for 3 minutes or until heated through. Drain well and allow to cool.
2 Put the ham onto a non-stick baking tray and cook under a grill preheated to high until slightly crisp.
3 Put the potatoes, peas, spring onions, tomatoes and herbs into a bowl and mix gently to combine.
4 Put the mayonnaise, yoghurt and mustard into a bowl and whisk gently to combine. Add to the salad and toss to coat. Top the salad with the shredded ham and serve with crusty bread. Serves 6

per serve I **fat 2.5 g** I **protein 10.5 g** I **carbohydrate 31 g** I **fibre 7 g** I **cholesterol 10.5 mg** I **energy 815 kJ (195 Cal)**

1 kg (2 lb) baby potatoes, unpeeled and quartered
1 cup (150 g/5 oz) fresh or frozen peas
100 g (3$^1/_3$ oz) shaved 97% fat-free ham
3 spring onions (scallions), sliced
150 g (5 oz) semi-dried tomatoes
2 tablespoons chopped fresh herbs (parsley and chives)
2 tablespoons reduced-fat mayonnaise
$^1/_4$ cup (60 ml/2 fl oz) reduced-fat Greek-style plain yoghurt
1 tablespoon wholegrain honey mustard

CHICKEN SCHNITZEL

2 small (420 g/14 oz) skinless
  chicken breasts
4 egg whites, lightly beaten
2 cups (150 g/5 oz) dry
  breadcrumbs
olive oil spray
1 medium Lebanese cucumber,
  unpeeled and chopped
1 clove garlic, crushed
100 g (3^1/$_3$ oz) reduced-fat
  Greek-style plain yoghurt
2 cups (115 g/3^2/$_3$ oz) shredded
  lettuce
2 medium tomatoes, sliced
4 large flour tortillas, 20 cm (8 in)
  diameter

1 Preheat oven to 220°C (425°F/Gas 7).
2 Cut the chicken breasts in half through the center.
Put each piece between 2 pieces of plastic wrap
and pound until flattened.
3 Dip the chicken pieces, one at a time, into the
egg whites and then into the breadcrumbs. Press
the breadcrumbs onto the chicken.
4 Lightly spray the chicken on both sides with olive
oil spray and bake, turning once, for 15 minutes or
until crisp and golden.
5 Combine the cucumber, garlic and yoghurt.
6 Serve the schnitzels topped with the lettuce and
tomatoes and cucumber mixture, wrapped in the
tortillas. Serves 4

**per serve | fat 10.5 g | protein 37.5 g | carbohydrate
48 g | fibre 4.5 g | cholesterol 73 mg | energy 1860 kJ
(445 Cal)**

chicken schnitzel

DINNER

teriyaki pork & noodle stir fry

TERIYAKI PORK & NOODLE STIR FRY

500 g (1 lb) lean pork fillet, thinly
   sliced
3 spring onions (scallions), sliced
350 g (12 oz) asparagus, cut into
   5 cm (2 in) pieces
200 g (6¹/₂ oz) snowpeas
200 g (6¹/₂ oz) broccoli, cut into
   florets
¹/₄ cup (60 ml/2 fl oz) water
350 g (12 oz) fresh udon noodles
¹/₄ cup (60 ml/2 fl oz) teriyaki
   marinade
2 teaspoons honey

1 Heat a non-stick wok until hot, add the pork in batches and stir fry over high heat until browned. Remove all the pork from the wok.

2 Add the spring onions, asparagus, snowpeas, broccoli and water to the wok. Cook until the vegetables are bright green and all the water has evaporated.

3 Separate the noodles and add to the wok with the pork, teriyaki marinade and honey. Cook until the sauce is heated through. Serves 4

per serve | fat 3.5 g | protein 36.5 g | carbohydrate 21.5 g | fibre 5.5 g | cholesterol 119 mg | energy 1105 kJ (265 Cal)

FISH FINGERS WITH TINY TATERS

500 g (1 lb) new potatoes, cut into
   wedges
olive oil spray
500 g (1 lb) skinless white fish
   fillets (whiting, flathead, perch)
4 egg whites, lightly beaten
1¹/₂ cups (160 g/5¹/₃ oz) cornflake
   crumbs
3 tablespoons plum sauce
1 tablespoon lime juice
1 teaspoon fish sauce

1 Preheat oven to 200°C (400°F/Gas 6). Line 2 baking trays with baking paper.

2 Put the potatoes into a baking dish, lightly spray with olive oil spray and bake for 40 minutes or until crisp and golden.

3 Cut the fish into strips 10 cm x 3 cm (4 in x 1 ¹/₄ in). Dip the fish strips, one at a time, into the egg whites and toss to coat in the cornflake crumbs. Arrange on the prepared trays. Lightly spray with olive oil spray and bake for 15 minutes or until crisp and golden.

4 Put the plum sauce, lime juice and fish sauce into a bowl and whisk to combine.

5 Serve the fish fingers with the potatoes, dipping sauce and a crisp green salad. Serves 4

per serve | fat 2.5 g | protein 36 g | carbohydrate 59.5 g | fibre 4 g | cholesterol 71 mg | energy 1715 kJ (410 Cal)

fish fingers with tiny taters

baked bean burgers

BAKED BEAN BURGERS

1 Put the beef mince, baked beans, egg white, breadcrumbs and parsley into a bowl and mix well to combine. Shape the mixture into 4 flat patties.
2 Lightly spray a non-stick fry pan or barbecue flatplate with canola oil spray. Cook the patties over medium heat for 15 minutes, turning once.
3 Place a slice of cheese on top of each pattie and cook for 5 minutes or until the cheese melts slightly and the patties are cooked through.
4 Toast the bread rolls and top with the lettuce, tomatoes, beetroot, a pattie, pineapple and tomato sauce. Serves 4
per serve I fat 14 g I protein 44 g I carbohydrate 57.5 g I fibre 10.5 g I cholesterol 73.5 mg I energy 2235 kJ (535 Cal)

500 g (1 lb) lean beef mince
260 g (8$^1/_3$ oz) can reduced-salt baked beans
1 egg white, lightly beaten
1 cup (70 g/2$^1/_4$ oz) fresh breadcrumbs
1 tablespoon chopped fresh parsley
canola oil spray
4 light processed cheddar cheese slices
4 medium (200 g/6$^1/_2$ oz) wholegrain bread rolls, halved
2 cups (115 g/3$^2/_3$ oz) shredded lettuce
2 medium tomatoes, sliced
4 slices canned beetroot
4 slices canned pineapple in natural juice, drained
$^1/_3$ cup (80 ml/2$^2/_3$ fl oz) tomato sauce

FUSS-FREE LASAGNE

500 g (1 lb) lean beef mince

2 cloves garlic, crushed

250 g (8 oz) button mushrooms, sliced

600 ml (19 fl oz) tomato pasta sauce

500 g (1 lb) fresh lasagne sheets

100 g (3⅓ oz) baby English spinach

200 g (6½ oz) low-fat ricotta cheese

150 ml (5 fl oz) can reduced-fat evaporated milk

½ cup (60 g/2 oz) grated reduced-fat cheddar cheese

1 Preheat oven to 200°C (400°F/Gas 6).

2 Heat a large non-stick fry pan, add the beef mince and cook over medium-high heat for 5 minutes or until browned.

3 Add the garlic, mushrooms and tomato pasta sauce and bring to the boil. Reduce the heat and simmer for 10 minutes.

4 Spoon ¼ cup (60 ml/2 fl oz) of the meat sauce into the bottom of a rectangular ovenproof dish. Top with a layer of lasagne sheets and half of the meat mixture.

5 Top with another layer of lasagne sheets, half of the spinach leaves and the combined ricotta and evaporated milk. Follow with another layer of lasagne sheets. Continue layering with the remaining ingredients, finishing with a layer of lasagne sheets topped with spinach and the ricotta mixture.

6 Sprinkle with the grated cheese and bake for 30-40 minutes or until the cheese is golden and the lasagne sheets are cooked through. Serves 8

per serve I **fat 9 g** I **protein 24 g** I **carbohydrate 21.5 g** I **fibre 3.5 g** I **cholesterol 49 mg** I **energy 1095 kJ (260 Cal)**

fuss-free lasagne

quick chicken phad thai

QUICK CHICKEN PHAD THAI

1 Put the rice noodles into a bowl, cover with boiling water and stand for 10 minutes or until the noodles are soft. Drain well.

2 Lightly spray a non-stick wok with canola oil spray and cook the chicken over high heat until browned.

3 Add the spring onions, carrot, zucchini and water and stir fry for 3 minutes.

4 Push the chicken and vegetables to one side and add the chives and eggs. Stir gently until the eggs start to scramble.

5 Add the noodles and sauces to the wok and stir fry until heated through. Remove from the heat and toss through the bean sprouts and coriander.

Serves 6

per serve I fat 5.5 g I protein 17 g I carbohydrate 31.5 g I fibre 2.5 g I cholesterol 95.5 mg I energy 1015 kJ (245 Cal)

* Replace the sweet chilli sauce with extra tomato sauce if you prefer.

250 g (8 oz) rice stick noodles
canola oil spray
300 g (10 oz) skinless chicken breasts, thinly sliced
2 spring onions (scallions), sliced
1 medium carrot, sliced
2 medium zucchini (courgette), sliced
2 tablespoons water
2 tablespoons chopped fresh garlic chives
2 eggs, lightly beaten
1 tablespoon fish sauce
1 tablespoon sweet chilli sauce*
2 tablespoons tomato sauce
1 cup (90 g/3 oz) bean sprouts
2 tablespoons chopped fresh coriander (cilantro)

HEARTY BEEF & POTATO PIE

8 sheets filo pastry

olive oil spray

500 g (1 lb) lean beef mince

1 medium onion, chopped

1 medium carrot, chopped

1 celery stick, chopped

200 g (6½ oz) button mushrooms, sliced

1 cup (150 g/5 oz) fresh or frozen peas

2 tablespoons plain flour

2 tablespoons Worcestershire sauce

2 tablespoons tomato sauce

1 cup (250 ml/8 fl oz) reduced-salt beef stock

500 g (1 lb) potatoes, peeled and chopped

¼ cup (60 ml/2 fl oz) skim or no-fat milk

2 tablespoons reduced-fat canola margarine

salt and pepper

1 Preheat oven to 200°C (400°F/Gas 6).

2 Line a 20 cm (8 in) pie dish with a sheet of filo, lightly spray with olive oil spray and top with another sheet of filo. Continue layering and spraying with the remaining pastry, allowing the excess pastry to overhang the side of dish. Roll up the excess pastry to sit on the rim of the pie. Bake for 20 minutes or until the pastry is crisp and golden.

3 Meanwhile, heat a large non-stick fry pan over high heat. Add the mince and onion and cook for 5 minutes or until the mince is browned and the onion is soft. Add the carrot, celery, mushrooms and peas and cook for 5 minutes or until soft. Add the flour and cook, stirring, for 1 minute. Add the sauces and stock and stir until the sauce boils and thickens slightly. Reduce the heat and simmer for 5 minutes. Remove from the heat and cool slightly.

4 Cook the potatoes in a large pan of boiling water for 15 minutes or until tender. Drain well, return to the pan and cook over low heat until all the moisture has evaporated. Remove from the heat, add the milk and margarine and mash until smooth and creamy. Season with salt and pepper.

5 Spoon the mince mixture into the pastry and top with the potato. Run a fork through the potato. Bake for 20 minutes or until the potato is golden. Serves 8

per serve I **fat 8.5 g** I **protein 19 g** I **carbohydrate 24 g** I **fibre 3.5 g** I **cholesterol 32 mg** I **energy 1045 kJ (250 Cal)**

hearty beef & potato pie

mexican meal in a basket

MEXICAN MEAL IN A BASKET

1 Put a tortilla into a 20 cm (8 in) round cake tin, lightly spray with olive oil spray and place under a grill preheated to high until crisp and firm enough to hold a basket shape. When the inside is cooked, shape the basket over the outside of the tin and grill until crisp. Repeat with the remaining tortillas.
2 Put the chicken breasts into a shallow fry pan, cover with water and simmer over low heat for 15 minutes or until the chicken is tender. Remove from the water and cool on absorbent paper. Finely shred the chicken.
3 Fill the tortilla baskets with the lettuce, carrot, tomato and combined corn and kidney beans. Top with the chicken, yoghurt, salsa and grated cheese.
Serves 4
per serve I **fat 11.5 g** I **protein 34.5 g** I **carbohydrate 33.5 g** I **fibre 6.5 g** I **cholesterol 78 mg** I **energy 1590 kJ (380 Cal)**

4 large flour tortillas, 30 cm (12 in) diameter
olive oil spray
2 small (420 g/14 oz) skinless chicken breasts
2 cups (115 g/3²⁄₃ oz) shredded lettuce
1 medium carrot, grated
1 medium tomato, chopped
130 g (4¹⁄₂ oz) can corn kernels, drained
300 g (10 oz) can red kidney beans, rinsed and drained
100 g (3¹⁄₃ oz) reduced-fat Greek-style plain yoghurt
100 g (3¹⁄₃ oz) mild tomato salsa
¹⁄₃ cup (40 g/1¹⁄₃ oz) grated reduced-fat cheddar cheese

BIG BAKED POTATOES

4 large (740 g/1 lb 7 oz) unpeeled potatoes

CHICKEN AND CORN TOPPING
2 cups (300 g/10 oz) shredded cooked skinless chicken breast
2 spring onions (scallions), sliced
130 g (4½ oz) can creamed corn
200 g (6½ oz) reduced-fat cottage cheese
100 g (3⅓ oz) reduced-fat Greek-style plain yoghurt
2 tablespoons snipped fresh chives
salt and pepper

SWEET CHILLI TUNA TOPPING
400 g (13 oz) chunk-style tuna in spring water, drained
2 spring onions (scallions), sliced
1 medium tomato, chopped
2 gherkins, chopped
¼ cup (60 ml/2 fl oz) sweet chilli sauce or tomato sauce
1 tablespoon lemon juice
1 tablespoon chopped fresh coriander (cilantro)
salt and pepper
200 g (6½ oz) reduced-fat Greek-style plain yoghurt

1 Preheat oven to 200°C (400°F/Gas 6).

2 Lightly prick the potatoes with a fork and place onto the rack in the middle of the oven. Bake for 45 minutes or until soft. Cut a cross in the top of each potato and push up the sides to make room for the filling.

3 Meanwhile, make your choice of filling. To make the chicken and corn topping, put the chicken, spring onions, creamed corn, cottage cheese, yoghurt and chives into a bowl and mix to combine. Season with salt and pepper. Spoon into the top of each potato.

4 To make the sweet chilli tuna topping, put the tuna, spring onions, tomato, gherkins, sweet chilli sauce, lemon juice and coriander into a bowl and mix to combine. Season with salt and pepper. Spoon a large dollop of yoghurt into the top of each potato and top with the tuna mixture. Serves 4

per serve (chicken and corn topping) I fat 6.5 g
I protein 34 g I carbohydrate 33 g I fibre 5 g
I cholesterol 68 mg I energy 1395 kJ (335 Cal)
per serve (tuna topping) I fat 3 g I protein 25.5 g
I carbohydrate 34 g I fibre 5 g I cholesterol 43 mg
I energy 1145 kJ (275 Cal)

big baked potatoes

lamb kebabs with couscous

LAMB KEBABS WITH COUSCOUS

1 Soak 8 bamboo skewers in water for 15 minutes.
2 Thread the lamb, spring onions, cherry tomatoes, mushrooms and zucchini onto the skewers. Place into a shallow non-metallic dish.
3 Whisk together the salad dressing and mint sauce, pour over the kebabs and set aside for 15 minutes. Cook on a lightly oiled preheated barbecue chargrill or flatplate, turning several times, for 10 minutes or until the meat is tender.
4 Meanwhile, put the couscous into a bowl, pour over the hot stock and set aside for 10 minutes or until the liquid has been absorbed. Separate the couscous with a fork and mix through the parsley.
5 Serve the kebabs with couscous. Serves 4

per serve | fat 4 g | protein 25.5 g | carbohydrate 46.5 g | fibre 4 g | cholesterol 49 mg | energy 1375 kJ (330 Cal)

300 g (10 oz) trim lamb loin, cut
    into 2 cm (3/4 in) cubes
4 spring onions (scallions), chopped
200 g (6 1/2 oz) cherry tomatoes
200 g (6 1/2 oz) small button
    mushrooms
200 g (6 1/2 oz) zucchini
    (courgette), thickly sliced
1/2 cup (125 ml/4 fl oz) fat-free
    Italian salad dressing
1 tablespoon mint sauce
1 cup (185 g/6 oz) couscous
1 2/3 cups (415 ml/13 1/2 fl oz) hot
    reduced-salt chicken stock
2 tablespoons chopped fresh
    flat-leaf parsley

TUNA FRIED RICE

1 Heat the oils in a non-stick wok, add the spring onions, carrot and capsicum and stir fry over medium heat until the vegetables soften.
2 Add the asparagus, corn and peas and cook for 3 minutes or until heated through.
3 Add the tuna and rice and mix gently to combine. Add the soy sauce and stir fry for 5 minutes or until the rice is heated through. Serves 6

per serve | fat 4.5 g | protein 20 g | carbohydrate 48 g | fibre 5.5 g | cholesterol 25 mg | energy 1320 kJ (315 Cal)
* You will need 1 1/2 cups (230 g/7 1/4 oz) uncooked brown rice.

1 teaspoon sesame oil
1 teaspoon canola oil
3 spring onions (scallions), sliced
1 medium carrot, chopped
1 medium red capsicum (bell
    pepper), chopped
160 g (5 1/3 oz) asparagus, chopped
1 cup (200 g/6 1/2 oz) fresh or
    frozen corn kernels
1 cup (150 g/5 oz) fresh or frozen
    peas
400 g (13 oz) can chunk-style tuna
    in spring water, drained
4 cups (720 g/1 lb 7 oz) cold
    cooked brown rice*
2-3 tablespoons reduced-salt
    soy sauce

tuna fried rice

Publisher Jody Vassallo
General manager Claire Connolly
Recipes & styling Jody Vassallo
Photographer Ben Dearnley
Home economist Penelope Grieve
Recipe testing Judy Clarke
Props stylist Melissa Singer
Designer Annette Fitzgerald
Editor Justine Harding
Consultant dietitian Dr Susanna Holt

STYLING CREDITS:
Chee Soon & Fitzgerald (02) 9361 1031
Lincraft (03) 9525 8770
Made in Japan (02) 9410 3799
Mud Australia (02) 9518 0220
Orson & Blake (02) 9326 1155
Royal Doulton (02) 9499 1904
Tomkin (02) 9319 2993
Villeroy & Boch (02) 9975 3099
Wheel & Barrow (02) 9413 9530
© **Recipes** Jody Vassallo 2003
© **Photography** Ben Dearnley
© **Series design** Fortiori Publishing

PUBLISHED BY FORTIORI PUBLISHING:
PO Box 126 Nunawading BC
Victoria 3110 Australia
Phone: 61 3 9872 3855
Fax: 61 3 9872 5454
salesenquiries@fortiori.com.au
www.fortiori.com.au

order direct on (03) 9872 3855

This publication is copyright. No part may be reproduced, stored in a retrieval system or transmitted in any form or by any means whether electronic, mechanical, photocopied, recorded or otherwise without the prior written permission of the publisher. Australian distribution to newsagents and supermarkets by Gordon and Gotch Ltd, 68 Kingsgrove Road, Belmore, NSW 2192.

Printed by McPherson's Printing Group.
Printed in Australia.

ISBN 0 9581609 3 7

DISCLAIMER: The nutritional information listed under each recipe does not include the nutrient content of garnishes or any accompaniments not listed in specific quantities in the ingredient list. The nutritional information for each recipe is an estimate only, and may vary depending on the brand of ingredients used and with natural biological variations in the composition of natural foods such as meat, fish, fruit and vegetables. The nutritional information was calculated by a qualified dietitian using FoodWorks dietary analysis software (Version 3, Xyris Software Pty Ltd, Highgate Hill, Queensland, Australia) based on the Australian food composition tables and food manufacturers' data. Where not specified, ingredients are always analysed as average or medium, not small or large. All recipes were analysed using 59 g eggs.

IMPORTANT: Those who might suffer particularly adverse effects from salmonella food poisoning (the elderly, pregnant women, young children and those with immune system problems) should consult their general practitioner about consuming raw or undercooked eggs.